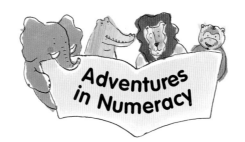

Adventures in Numeracy

The Number Team in the Jungle

Sally Hewitt

illustrated by Ruth Rivers

Thameside Press

Notes for parents and teachers
How to use this book

Each double page has a numeracy theme, such as counting in tens, time, or shapes.

The story —

Question boxes

Monkey's math tip

Question boxes

Each box has two questions. Elephant's questions are easier than Crocodile's. Start with Elephant's questions, then move on to Crocodile's. Or you can choose to answer only Elephant's or only Crocodile's questions. The answers are on page 30.

Monkey's math tip

Read Monkey's math tip for help with the Number Team's questions, or extra information about the math in the scene.

There are ideas for games and activities on page 31.

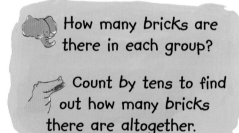

How many bricks are there in each group?

Count by tens to find out how many bricks there are altogether.

Counting by tens

When you count by tens, the unit always stays the same: 10, 20, 30, and so on.

When you start on 3 and count by tens, this happens: 3, 13, 23, 33, and so on.

Meet the Number Team

Crocodile, Lion, Monkey, and Elephant
are ready for a job in the jungle. They are
building a swimming pool, a playground,
and a basketball court for their friends,
but they need your help to finish the job!

First the Number Team unloads and counts all the materials.

How many bricks are there in each group?

Count by tens to find out how many bricks there are altogether.

Monkey has found 8 and 2 bricks to make 10. Which other patterns of 10 bricks can you see?

If you split 10 bricks into 3 piles, what patterns could you make?

What other groups of 10 things can you find?

Can you find 20, 30, 40, and 50 of the same thing?

Counting by tens

When you count by tens, the unit always stays the same: 10, 20, 30, and so on.

When you start on 3 and count by tens, this happens: 3, 13, 23, 33, and so on.

"Hurry up, we have to dig the swimming pool by lunchtime," puffs Monkey.

Find all the tools that are used for digging.

Find all the digging tools with long handles.

Find all the tools that are not used for digging.

Find all the tools with short handles that are not used for digging.

Find all the tools that are used for cutting.

Think of different ways to sort the tools.

Sorting and sets

Spades, pickaxes, forks, and trowels belong to a set of digging tools.

Digging tools

Short-handled digging tools

You can sort the digging tools with short handles into a smaller set.

"When you've put up the umbrellas, come in for a swim!" shouts Elephant.

Find a diving board the same size, shape, and color as Monkey's.

Find all the matching pairs in and around the swimming pool.

Match the umbrellas to the tables that have the same color and pattern.

Find the umbrellas that do not match any of the tables.

Find groups of 2, 3, 4, and 5 stools.

Match the groups of stools to tables with the same number of places.

Matching

Things can be the same in all kinds of ways.

They can be the same number, size, shape, weight, color, or pattern. For example, an apple and an orange have different colors and tastes, but they have the same round shape.

Monkey can't wait to try out each swing for size.

Find the longest swing, the longest snake, and the longest growing creeper.

Point to the ladders in order of length, starting with the shortest.

Measuring

Estimate the size of things just by looking. Check your guess and become an expert! Use rulers for length and height, scales for weight, and a measuring jug for liquid.

How many times will Crocodile's tail fit along the red pole?

How much longer is the red pole than the yellow one? Use the hammers to measure them.

Which bucket in each pair would be the lightest to carry?

Three small stones are as heavy as one large rock. If Elephant can carry four large rocks, how many small stones can she carry?

"I can climb higher than you!" laughs Monkey.

If the green frog jumps along by twos, what numbers will it land on?

If the yellow frog jumps back by threes, what numbers will it land on?

If Lion climbs up 5 rungs, what number will he be on?

If Monkey climbs down 4 rungs, what number will she be on?

Counting forward and back

Write out a 50-number line. Then use it for adding and taking away.

26+7   Put your finger on 26 and move it along 7 numbers. You will land on the answer.

43-5   Put your finger on 43 and move it back 5 places to find the answer.

Start on different rungs and go up 3 every time. Which numbers do you land on?

Start on different rungs and go down 3 every time. Which numbers do you land on?

"Lunchtime! Who wants some pizza?" calls Lion.

How many bananas has Monkey eaten? Double the number to find how many she will eat altogether.

Elephant has picked 50 bananas. Double the number to find how many she will pick altogether.

Double and half

You can halve a number by dividing it by 2. Find half of 10 by doing the sum 10 ÷ 2.

You can double a number by multiplying it by 2. Double 5 by doing the sum 5 × 2.

Crocodile has eaten half of the apples. How many were there to start with?

Lion wants half of the oranges. How many will he eat?

How will Lion share 2 pizzas among 4 animals?

How could Lion give them all some mushroom and some tomato pizza?

"Time to tidy up," says Crocodile after lunch.

1:00

What time is it now?

What time will it be in 30 minutes? Which number will the long hand point to on the clock?

Who hasn't finished their job?

How many minutes did Lion, Monkey, and Elephant take?

1:10

1:03

1:20

1:05

Who worked the fastest?
Who was the slowest?

Work starts again at half past one. How long does Crocodile have to pick up the apple cores?

Telling the time

When the time is something o'clock, the long hand always points to 12. On a digital clock, 4:00 the 2 numbers on the right side of the dots are always zeros.

When the time is half past something, the long hand always points to 6. On a digital clock, 4:30 the number on the right side of the dots is always 30.

17

The grandstand is nearly ready. "Do we need so many chairs?" groans Lion.

Count by fives to find how many red chairs Lion has put out.

Count by fours to find how many blue chairs Lion needs altogether.

Count by twos to find how many flowers Crocodile needs for the pots.

The number story of the flower pots is 2+2+2+2+2+2+2= 14. Can you tell the same story using the x sign?

How many leaves is Monkey putting in each strip? How many strips are there altogether?

How many different ways can you find to tell the number story of Monkey's leaves?

Counting by twos

When you add up 2 or more of the same number, you can do it quickly if you know your multiplication tables. So instead of 2+2+2+2+2+2+2+2+2+2=20, you can do it more quickly with the calculation 10×2=20.

Next they finish the basketball court. "Who made those footprints?" grumbles Crocodile.

Which waterproof sheet is big enough to cover the basketball court if it rains?

Lion has covered half of the court with wood. How much is there left to do?

How many square tiles will Monkey need to cover the front of the cupboard?

Why are the square tiles the best shape to cover the front of the cupboard?

How many planks of wood has Lion used so far?

How many more planks of wood will Lion need to finish the whole area?

Measuring area

Area means the size of a flat space. We measure area in squares. Cut out squares and use them to measure the area of a book or a table top. Then you can say how many squares make up the area of the book or table.

Elephant is having trouble putting up the flags in the right order.

Grand Opening

Which 5 shapes should Monkey paint next along the top of the banner?

What are the 3 missing shapes along the bottom of the banner?

22

Help Elephant find the next 6 flags in the pattern.

Choose a pattern for the colored balloons. See how many times you can make the pattern with Lion's balloons.

Find a different way to arrange the cakes.

Find as many ways of ordering the cakes as you can.

Patterns

To spot a missing number or shape, look for a pattern. The numbers 10, 20, ?, 40, 50 make a pattern of counting by tens, so the missing number is 30.

26, 24, 22, ?, 18 is a pattern of counting down by twos, so the missing number is 20.

23

"Where are all the paintbrushes?" asks Crocodile.

Elephant has spotted 2 brushes. How many more must she find?

Tell a number story about the brushes, first using + and then using –.

Number stories

You can tell number stories in different ways. For example:

Lion has 9 tiles. He finds 10 more to make 19 tiles altogether. This story makes the sum 9 + 10 = 19.

The story can be told in another way: There are 19 tiles on the list. 10 are missing, so Lion has 9 tiles. This makes the sum 19 – 10 = 9.

Find cubes and cuboids.

cube   cuboid

Say as many things as you can about cubes and cuboids.

How many different shapes can you find?

Which shapes are 2D (flat) and which are 3D (solid)?

2D and 3D shapes

Circles, squares, and triangles are flat, or 2D, shapes. You can measure them in two ways—how long and how wide they are.

Spheres, cubes, and pyramids are solid, or 3D, shapes. You can measure them in three ways—how long, how wide, and how high they are.

They all join in the fun at the grand opening.

Find five different 2D shapes.

Find five different 3D shapes.

Number stories

Numbers, shapes, sizes, and patterns are everywhere. Try to make up questions and number stories from things you see around you.

1 2 3 4 5 6 7 8 9 10 11 12 13 14 15 16 17 18 19 20

Answers

Elephant and Crocodile ask both open and closed questions. Closed questions have just one correct answer. Open questions have a number of different correct answers. These will encourage your child to think of alternative answers and, in some cases, to count all the different possibilities.

4–5 Counting by tens

🐘 10 bricks in each group.
🐊 60 bricks altogether.

🐘 5 and 5   6 and 4   7 and 3
   9 and 1   10 and 0.
🐊 Two possible patterns are:
   5, 3, and 2   7, 2, and 1.

🐘 Poles, buckets, tiles, spades, cement sacks.
🐊 20 cement sacks, 30 buckets,
   40 poles, 50 tiles.

6–7 Sorting and sets

🐘 Forks, spades, pickaxes, trowels,
   power shovel.
🐊 3 forks, 2 spades, 1 pickaxe.

🐘 Mallets, rakes, brooms, and shears.
🐊 3 mallets, 2 rakes, 1 broom, all the shears.

🐘 Shears are used for cutting.
🐊 One way to sort the tools is by the color
   of their handles (red, yellow, or blue).

8–9 Matching

🐘 The matching diving board is behind Lion.
🐊 Brown diving boards, cement sacks, green
   frogs, rubber rings, inflatable balls, red
   stools, paintbrushes, brooms, hammers,
   wheelbarrows, yellow and blue umbrellas.

🐘 Yellow and blue umbrella + small round table.
   Orange and white umbrella + triangular table.
   Green and white striped umbrella + large round
   table. Yellow and blue umbrella + square table.
🐊 The green umbrella with white spots and the
   light blue umbrella with red flowers.

🐘 2 red, 3 blue, 4 white, 5 yellow stools.
🐊 Red stools and small round table. Blue stools
   and triangular table. White stools and square
   table. Yellow stools and large round table.

10–11 Measuring

🐘 The swing to the right of Monkey. The red,
   blue, and white snake. The left-hand creeper.
🐊 Yellow, blue, green ladder.

🐘 3 times.
🐊 4 hammers longer.

🐘 Pink bucket of leaves. Blue bucket
   of flowers. Empty red bucket.
🐊 12 small stones.

12–13 Counting on and back

🐘 3, 5, 7, 9, 11, 13, 15, 17, 19.
🐊 16, 13, 10, 7, 4, 1.

🐘 Rung 10.
🐊 Rung 13.

🐘 If you start on 3: 3, 6, 9, 12, 15, 18.
🐊 If you start on 20: 20, 17, 14, 11, 8, 5, 2.

14–15 Doubling and halving

🐘 5 bananas. 10 altogether.
🐊 100 bananas altogether.

🐘 20 apples to start with.
🐊 9 oranges.

🐘 Half a pizza each.
🐊 A quarter of the mushroom pizza and
   a quarter of the tomato pizza each.

16–17 Time

🐘 One o'clock (1:00).
🐊 Half past one (1:30). The long hand
   will point to 6.

🐘 Crocodile hasn't finished.
🐊 3 minutes (Lion), 5 minutes (Elephant),
   10 minutes (Monkey).

🐘 Lion was fastest. Crocodile was slowest
   (because he didn't finish).
🐊 10 minutes.

18–19 Counting by twos, threes, fours, and fives

🐘 20 red chairs.
🐊 40 blue chairs altogether.

🐘 14 flowers.
🐊 7 x 2 = 14.

🐘 3 leaves in each strip. 6 strips altogether.
🐊 3+3+3+3+3+3=18, or 6 x 3 = 18.

20–21 Area

🐘 The yellow sheet will cover the court.
🐊 Half of the court left to cover.

🐘 8 square tiles.
🐊 They will cover the front of the cupboard
   without leaving any gaps.

🐘 12 planks of wood.
🐊 12 more planks of wood.

22–23 Patterns

🐘 Green square, red triangle, pink diamond,
   yellow circle, blue star.
🐊 Pink diamond, yellow circle, green square.

🐘 3 pink and yellow flags, 2 orange and
   blue flags, 1 green and blue flag.
🐊 One pattern could be: 3 blue, 2 red, 1 yellow.
   You could make this pattern 3 times.

🐘 One different way is: brown, yellow, pink.
🐊 There are six different ways altogether:
   1) yellow, pink, brown   4) brown, pink, yellow
   2) yellow, brown, pink   5) pink, brown, yellow
   3) brown, yellow, pink   6) pink, yellow, brown

24–25 Number bonds

🐘 13 paintbrushes.
🐊 2+13=15   15–13=2

🐘 4 hammers.
🐊 2+4=6   6–4=2

🐘 7 buckets.
🐊 3+7=10   10–7=3

26–27 Shapes

🐘 The clock face is a circle. The balls are spheres.
🐊 Circle: flat (2D); one curved edge; no corners.
   Sphere: solid (3D); curved surface; no corners.

🐘 The boxes are cubes and cuboids.
🐊 Cube: solid (3D); straight edges; 8 corners;
   each edge is the same length; 6 square faces.
   Cuboid: solid (3D); straight edges;
   8 corners; 6 rectangular faces.

🐘 Circles (clock face), spheres (balls), squares
   (flags), cubes (boxes), rectangles (flags),
   cuboids (ice cream tubs), triangles (flags),
   pyramids (weights), diamonds (kite), cones
   (megaphone), cylinders (rolled-up mats).
🐊 2D: circle, square, rectangle, triangle, diamond.
   3D: sphere, cube, cuboid, pyramid, cone, cylinder.

28–29 Shapes and numbers

🐘 Circles (clock face), triangles (table), squares
   (flags), rectangles (flags), stars (on flags).
🐊 Spheres (balls), pyramids (tent), cuboids
   (cake stand), ovoids (balloons), cylinders
   (rolled-up mat).

🐘 5 animals in each team.
🐊 3 cookies each.

🐘 11 red, 3 yellow (floating away), and 5 blue.
🐊 One story is: six turtles are waiting. Four are
   already on the slides. That makes ten in all.

Notes for parents and teachers
Games and activities

Use the Number Team's questions to help you find more math in the pictures. Then try these games and activities:

4–5 Counting by tens

Try counting by tens, starting from any number between 1 and 10 (7, 17, 27, and so on). Now start with any number between 90 and 100 and count backward by tens (96, 86, 76, and so on).

6–7 Sorting and sets

A group of toys is a set. Sort the toys into subsets. For example: toys you play with often, toys you hardly ever play with; toys with wheels, toys without wheels. Find different ways to sort clothes and shopping.

10–11 Measuring

Play guess and check. Guess how many drinking straws or matchsticks will fit across a table or around a newspaper. Check to see if you were right. Who made the most accurate guess?

16–17 Time

Use a watch to time how long it takes to do something. Ask a friend to time you making a sandwich or running between two trees, for example. Now time your friend. Who is the fastest?

18–19 Counting by twos, threes, fours, and fives

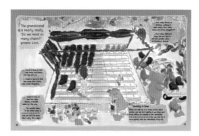

Make a 10 x 10 number grid (100 squares). Color in the squares you land on counting by twos. Use a different color for counting by fives. Make patterns counting by different numbers.

22–23 Patterns

Make up a repeating pattern using shapes, such as ❚❚▲●●❚❚▲●●. Use your pattern to make a bookmark with felt tip pens, paints, or potato prints.

26–27 Shapes

Boxes, balls, and cardboard rolls are interesting shapes. Discover as much as you can about each shape—its name, and how many faces, corners, and edges it has. Open it out flat to see the new shape it makes.

28–29 Number stories

Make up a number story, perhaps about children getting on and off a school bus. See if your friends can do the calculation as you tell the story. Who has the right answer at the end of the story?

Distributed in the United States by
Smart Apple Media
1980 Lookout Drive
North Mankato, MN 56003

Text by Sally Hewitt
Illustrations by Ruth Rivers

Series editor: Mary-Jane Wilkins
Editor: Russell McLean
Designer: John Jamieson
Educational consultant: Norma Penny, Barnett
    Infants School, Chessington, Surrey, U.K.

ISBN 1-930643-64-0

Library of Congress Control Number: 2001088846

Printed in China

9 8 7 6 5 4 3 2 1